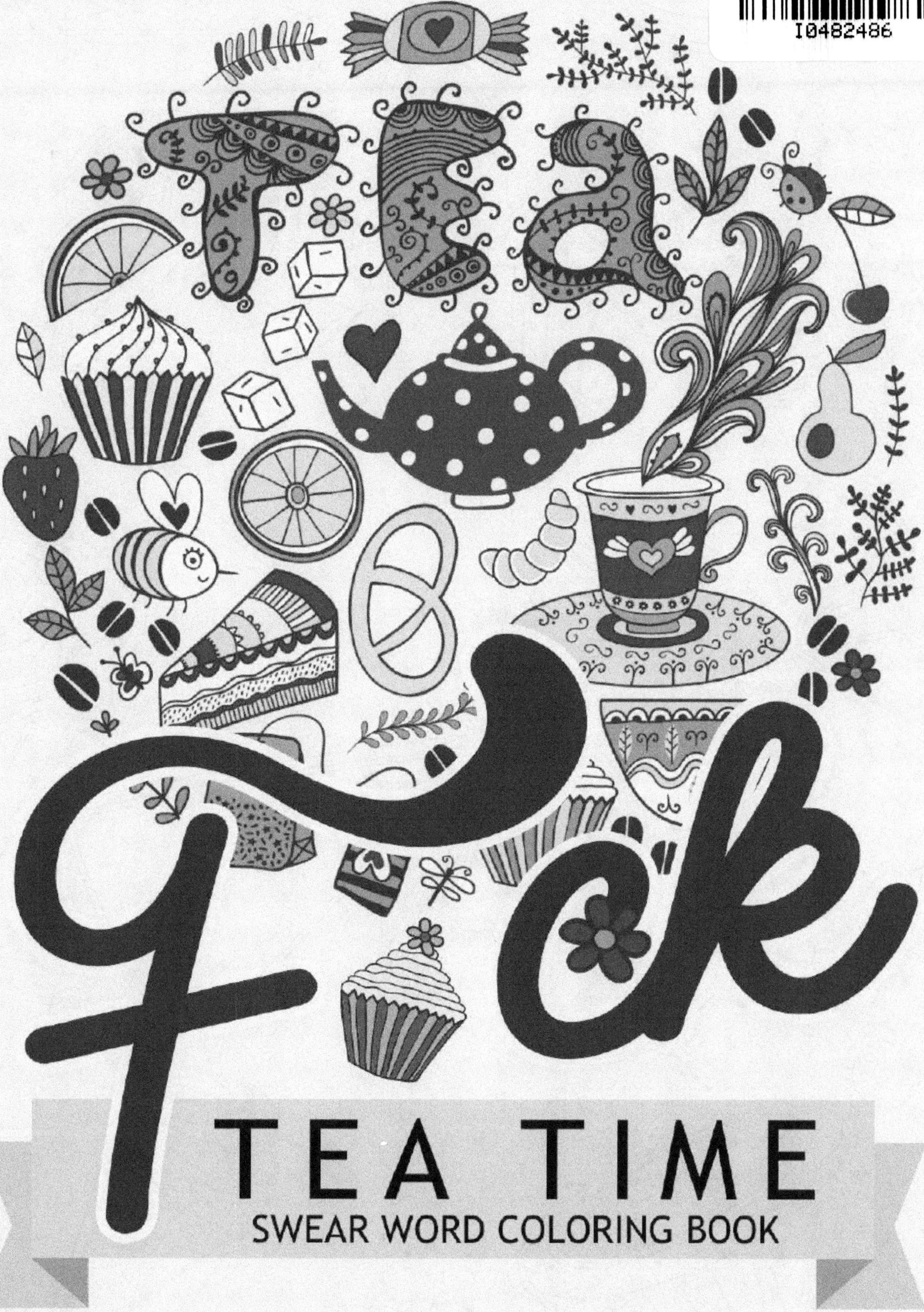

TEA TIME

SWEAR WORD COLORING BOOK

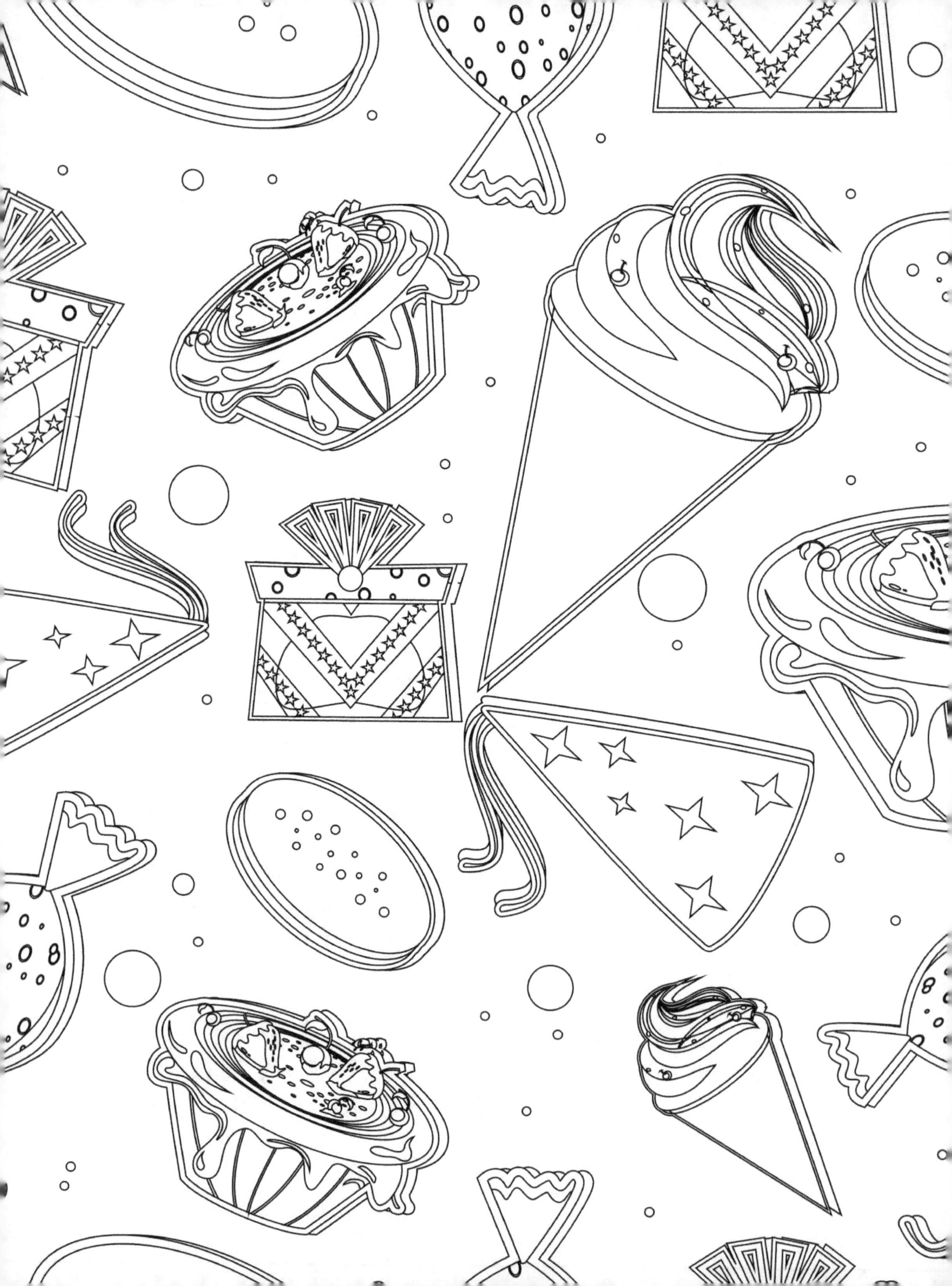

COLOR TEST PAGE

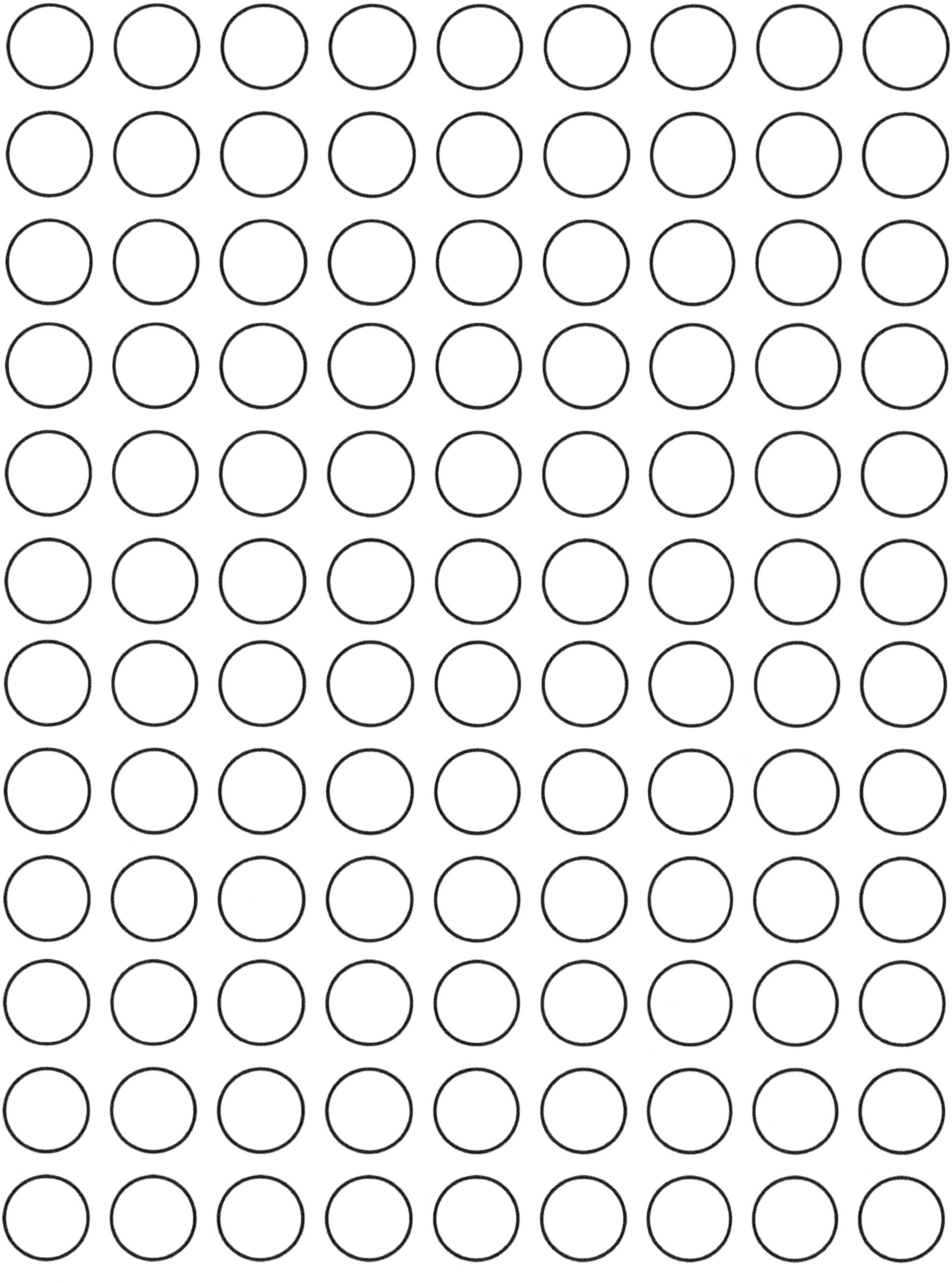

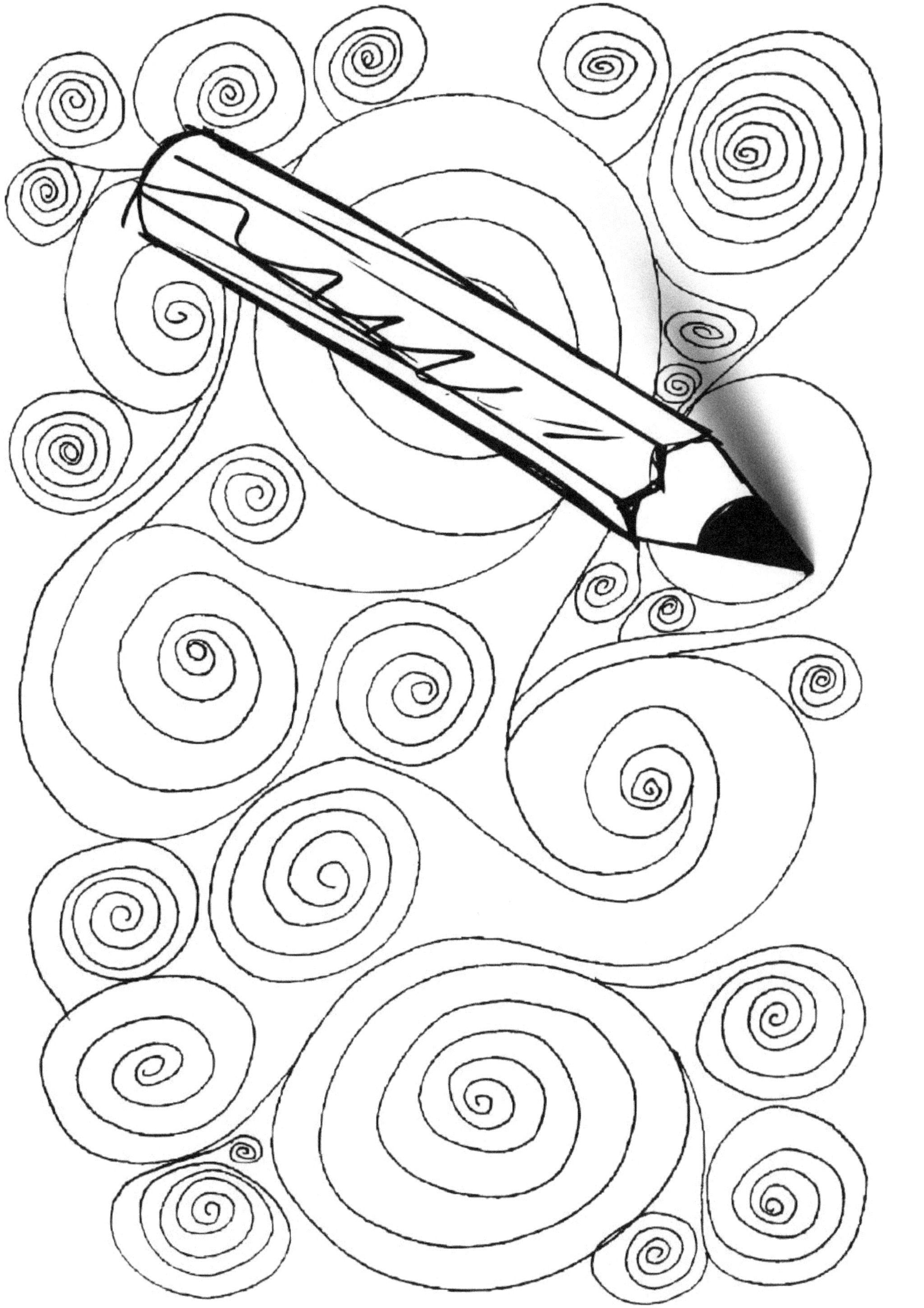

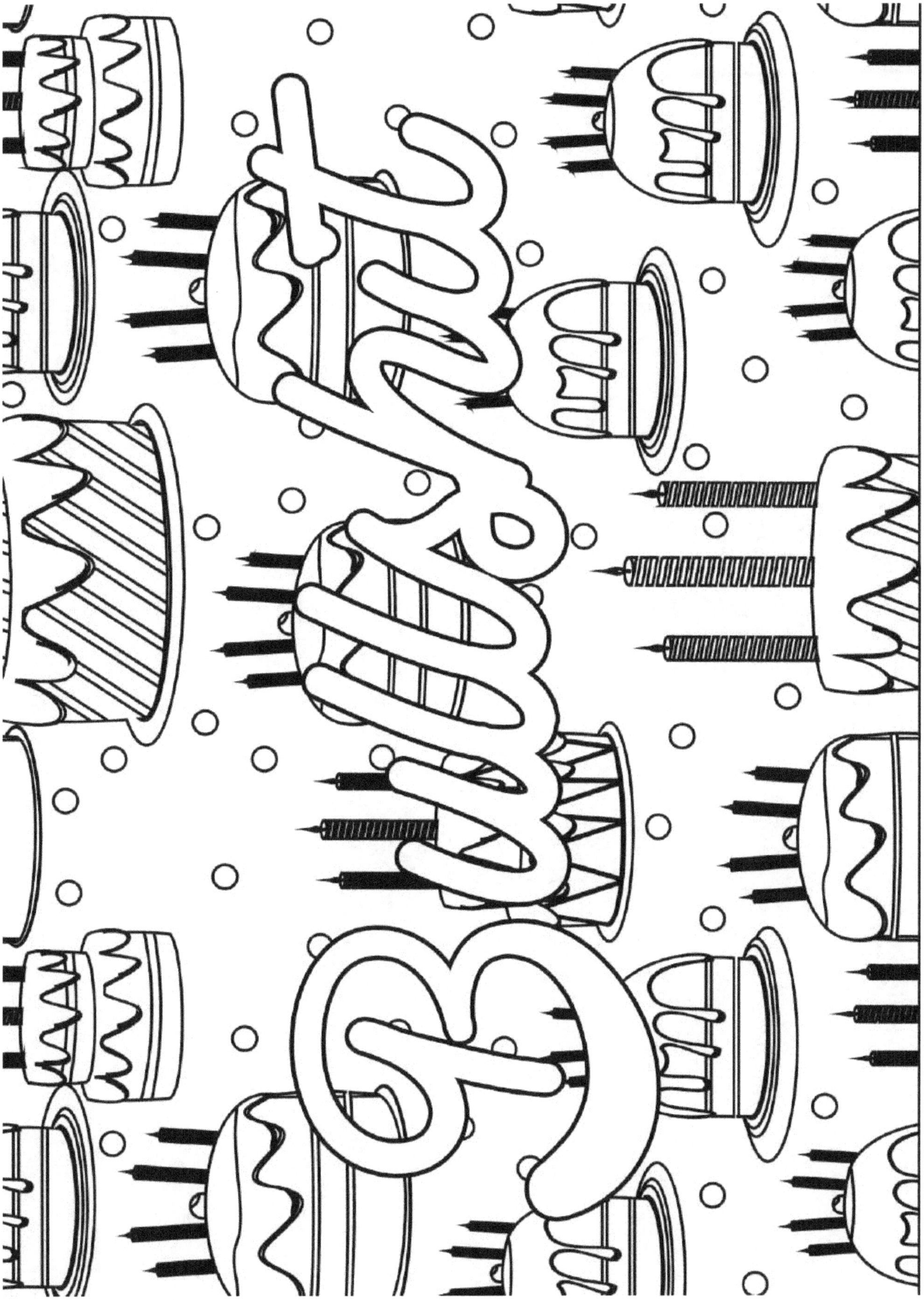

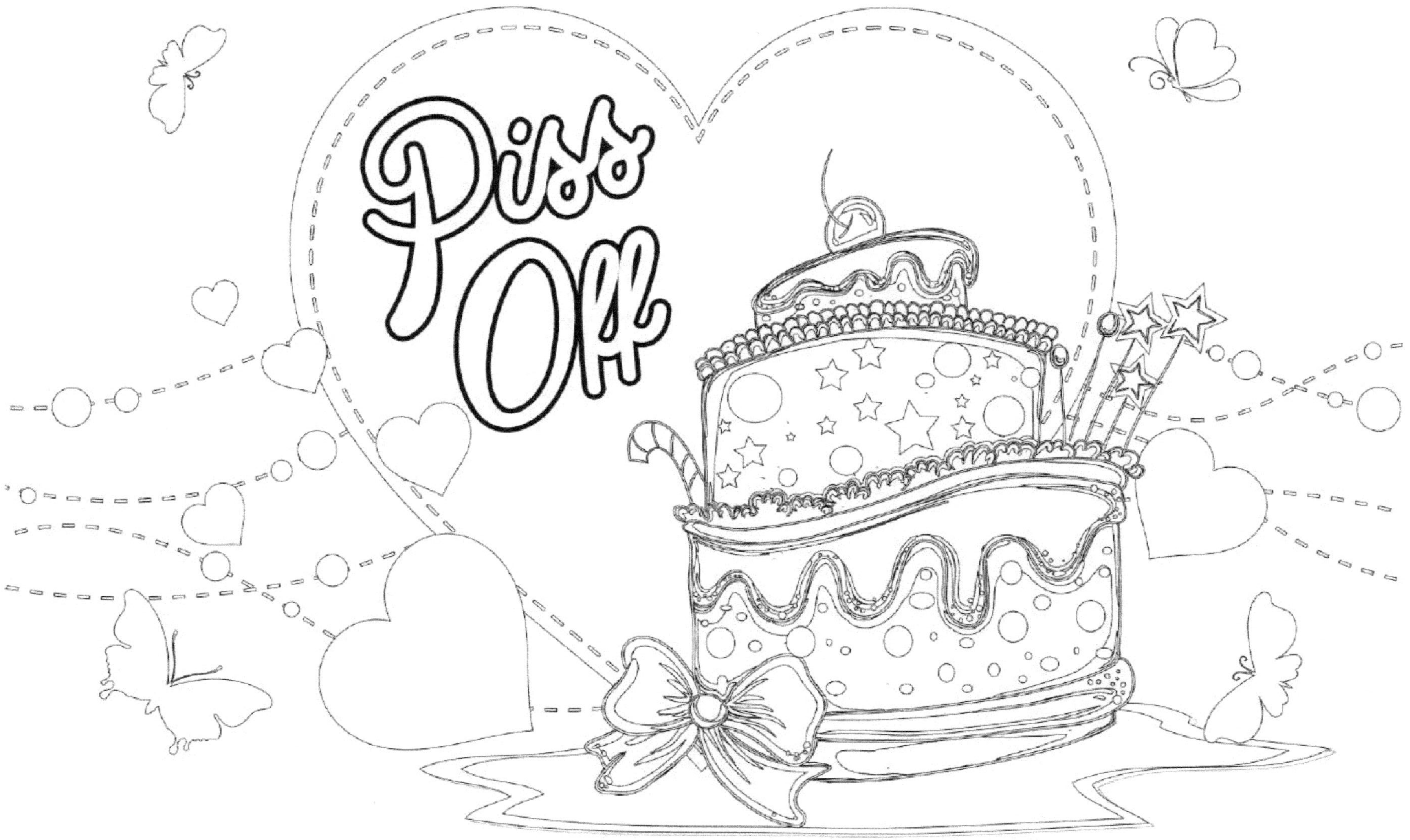
Piss Off

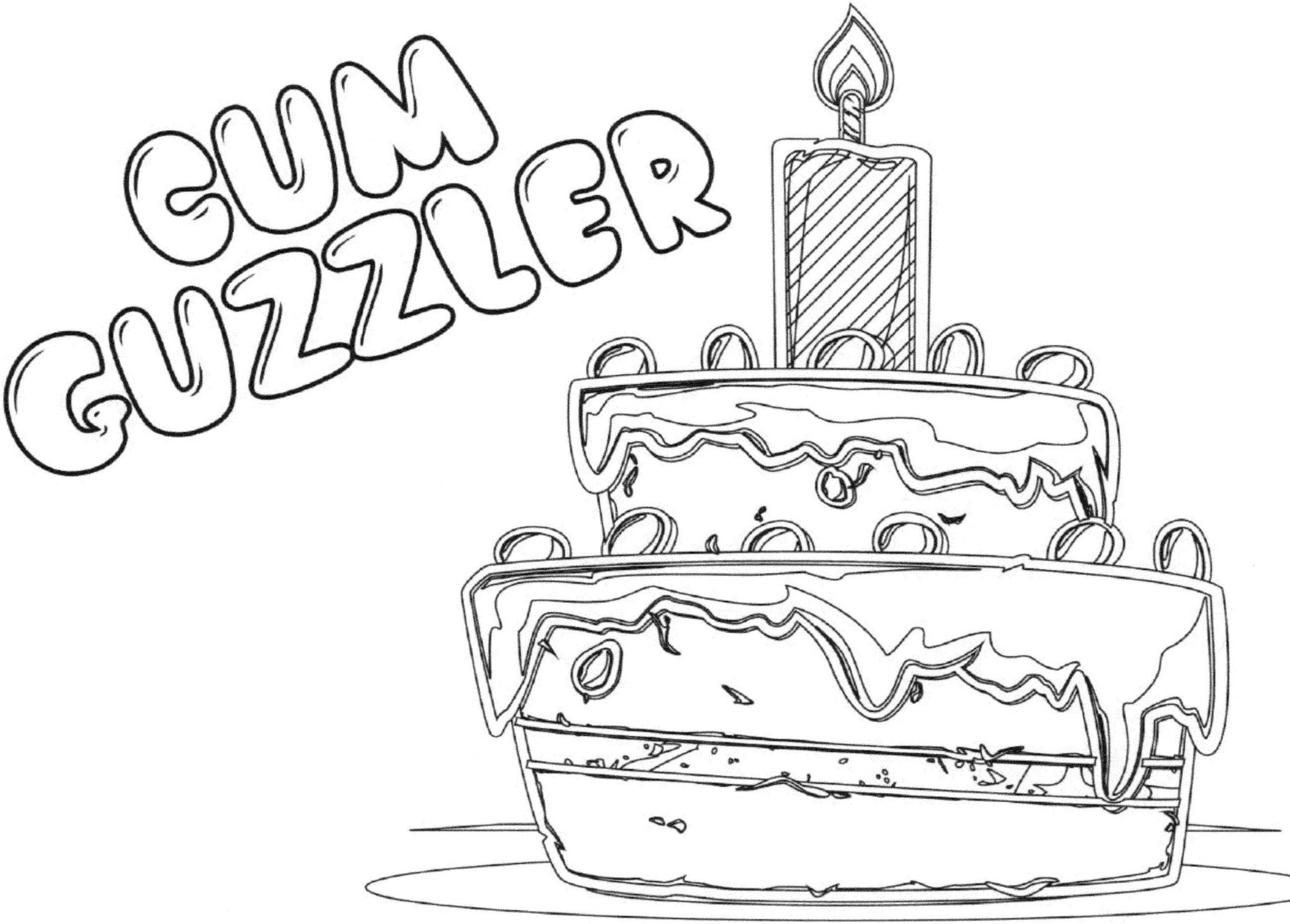
CUM
GUZZLER

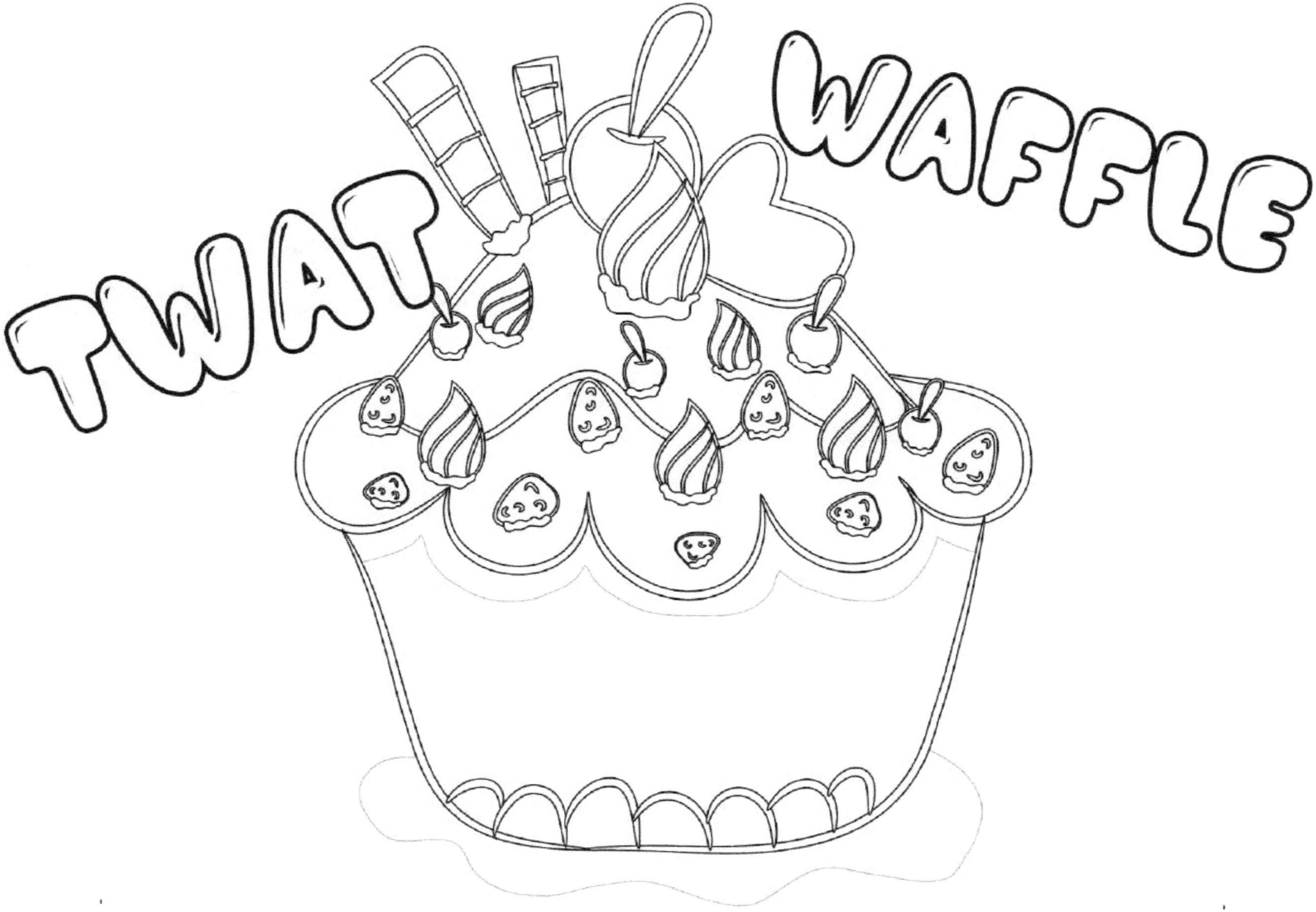
TWAT WAFFLE

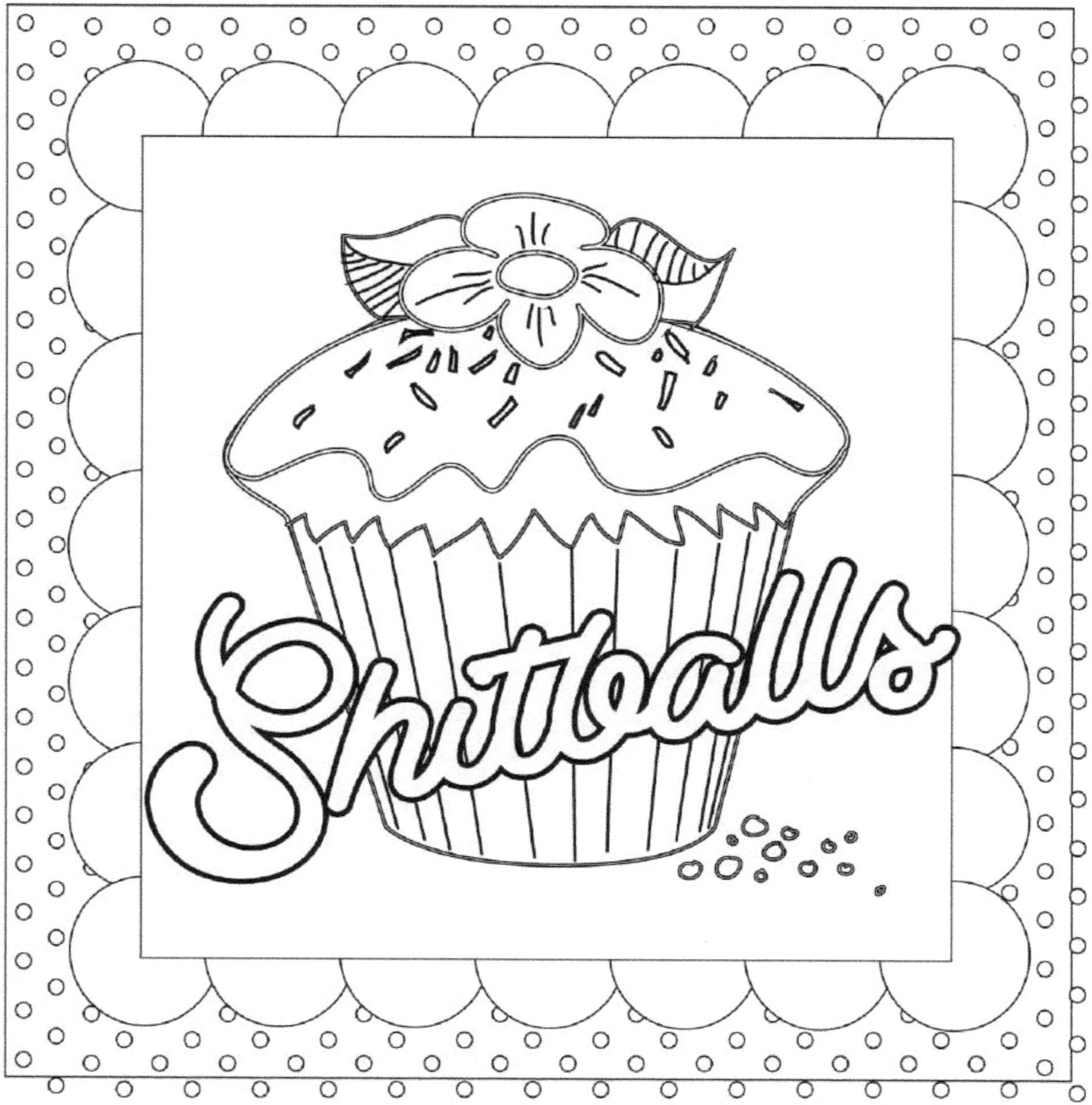
Shitballs

SUGAR TITS

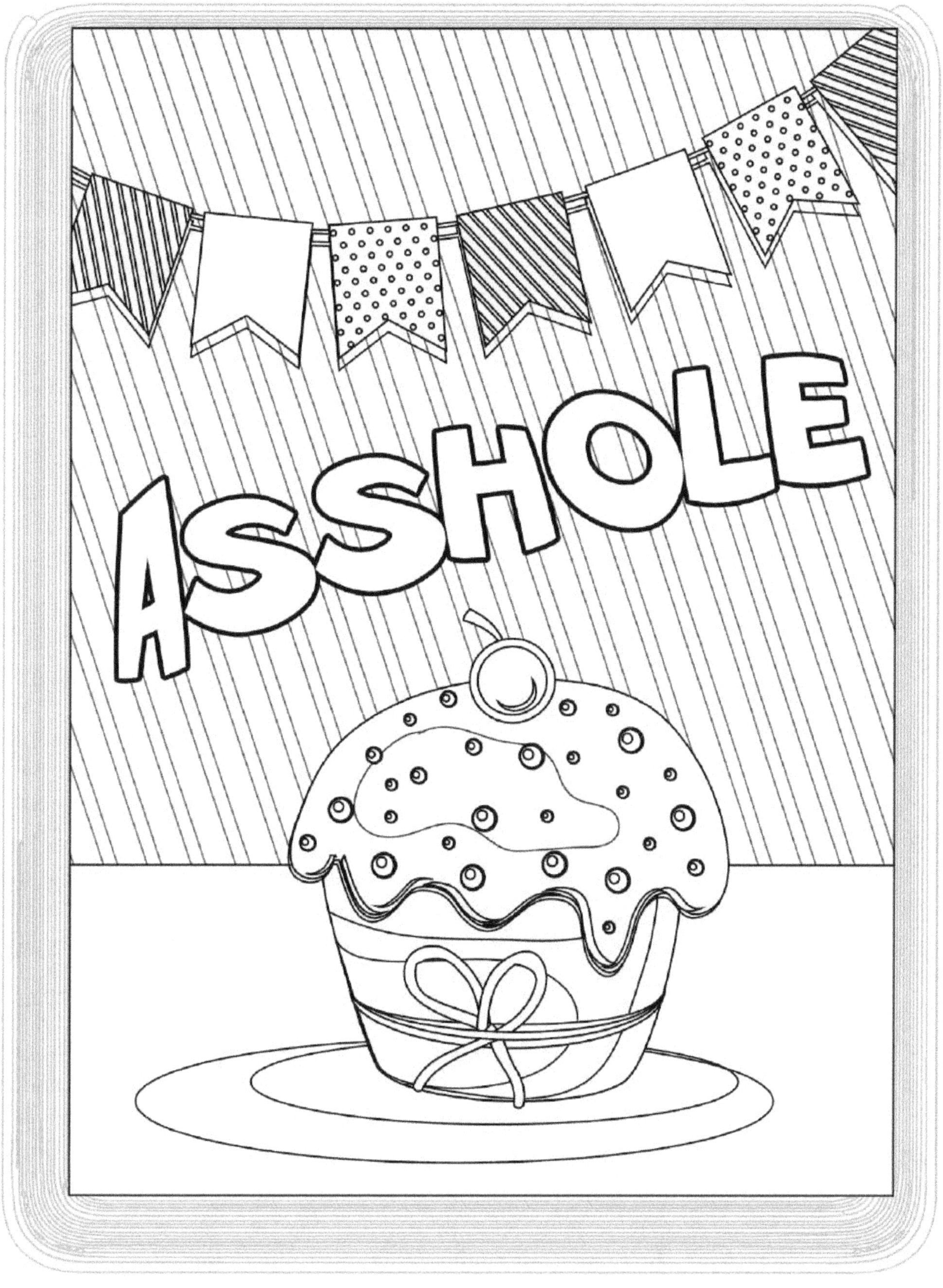
ASSHOLE

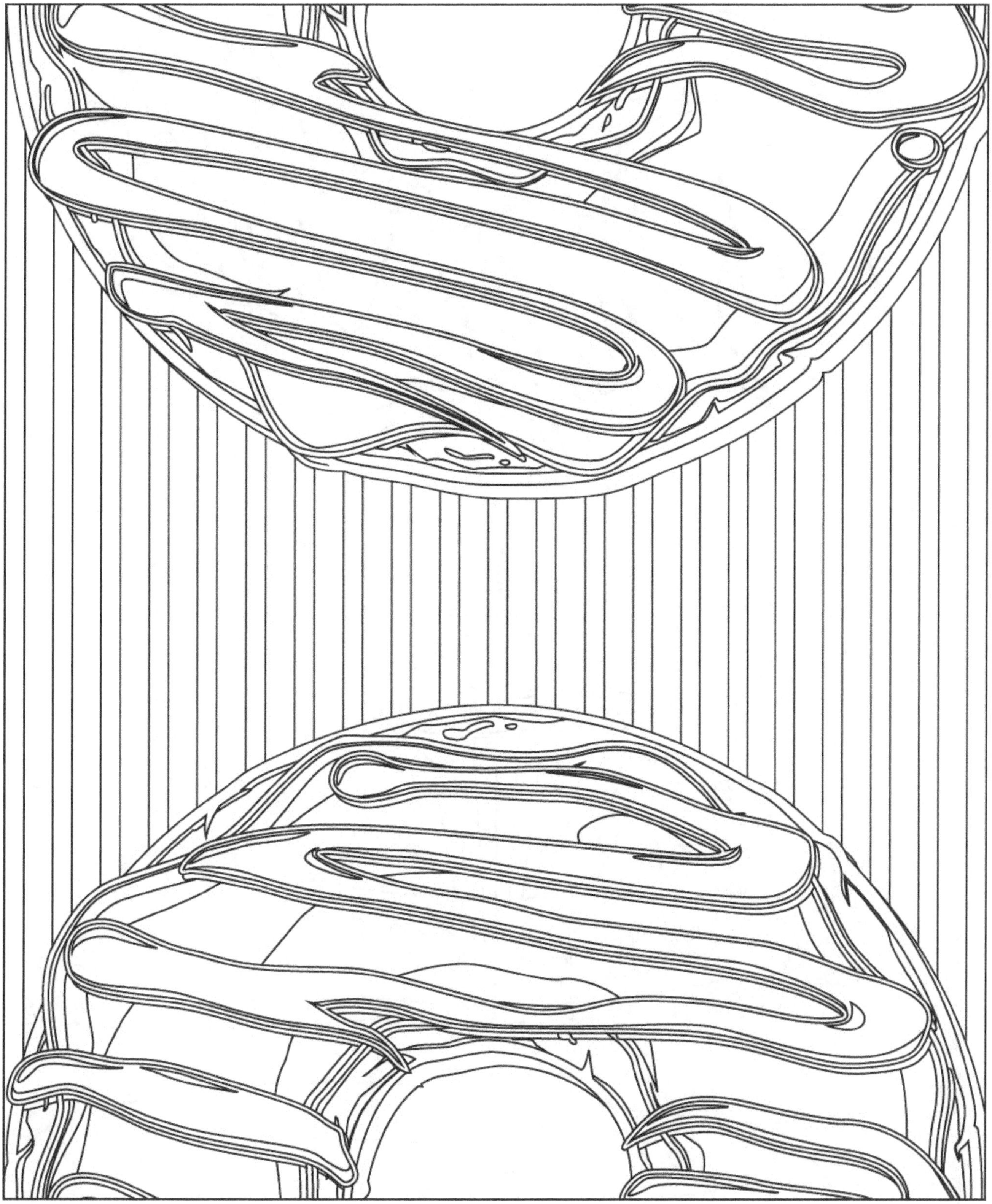

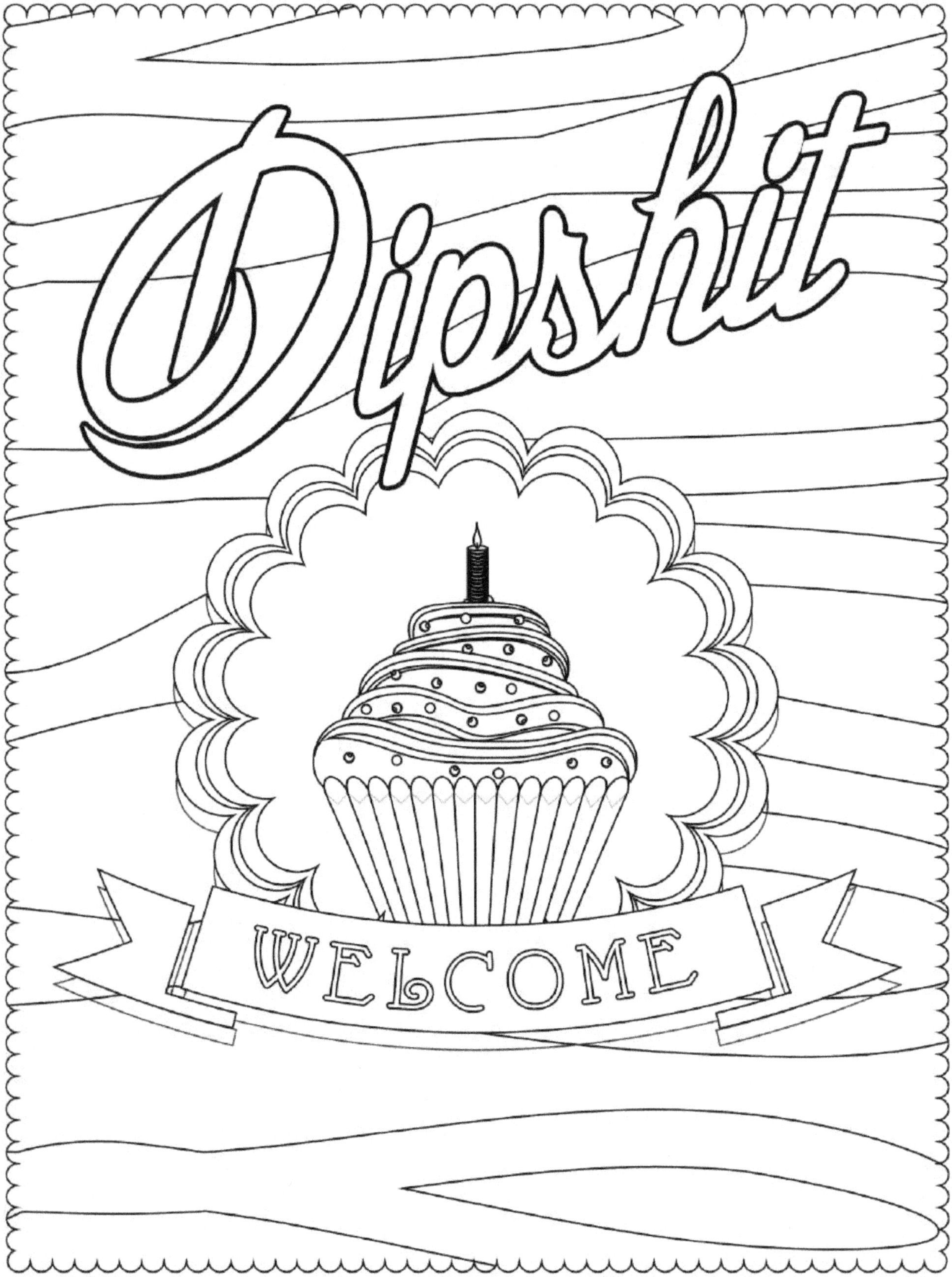
Dipshit
WELCOME

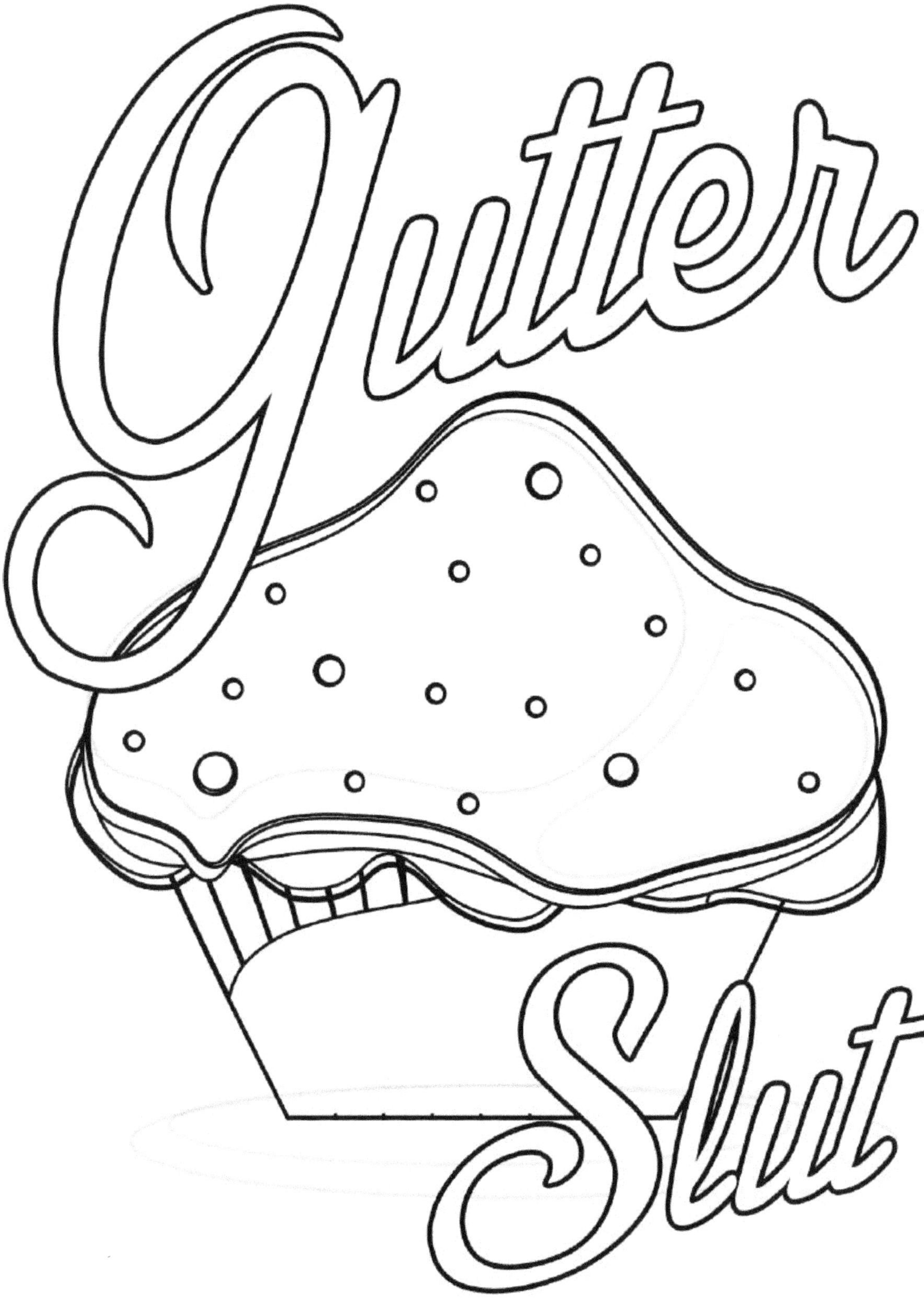
Gutter
Slut

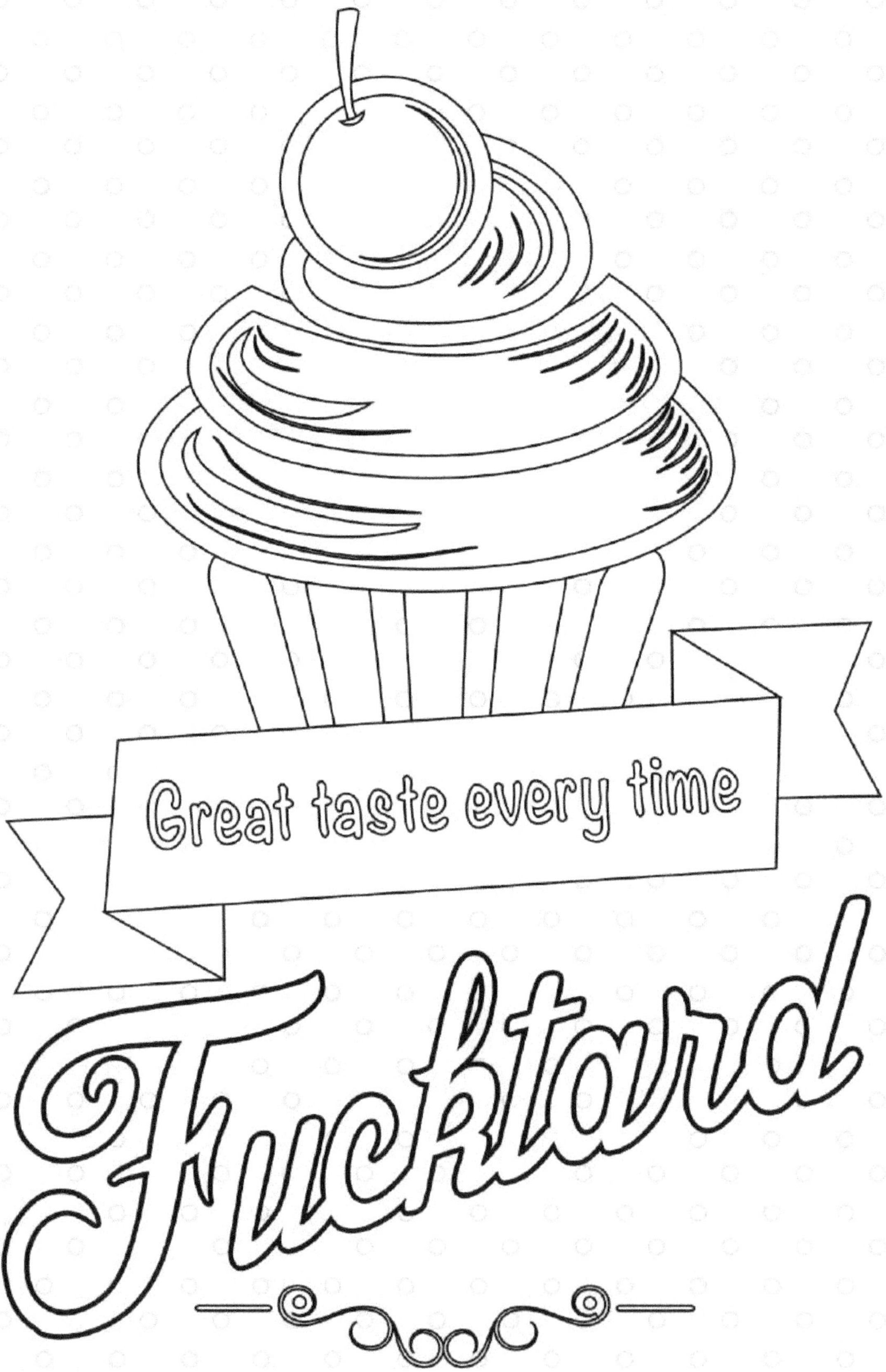
Great taste every time
Fucktard

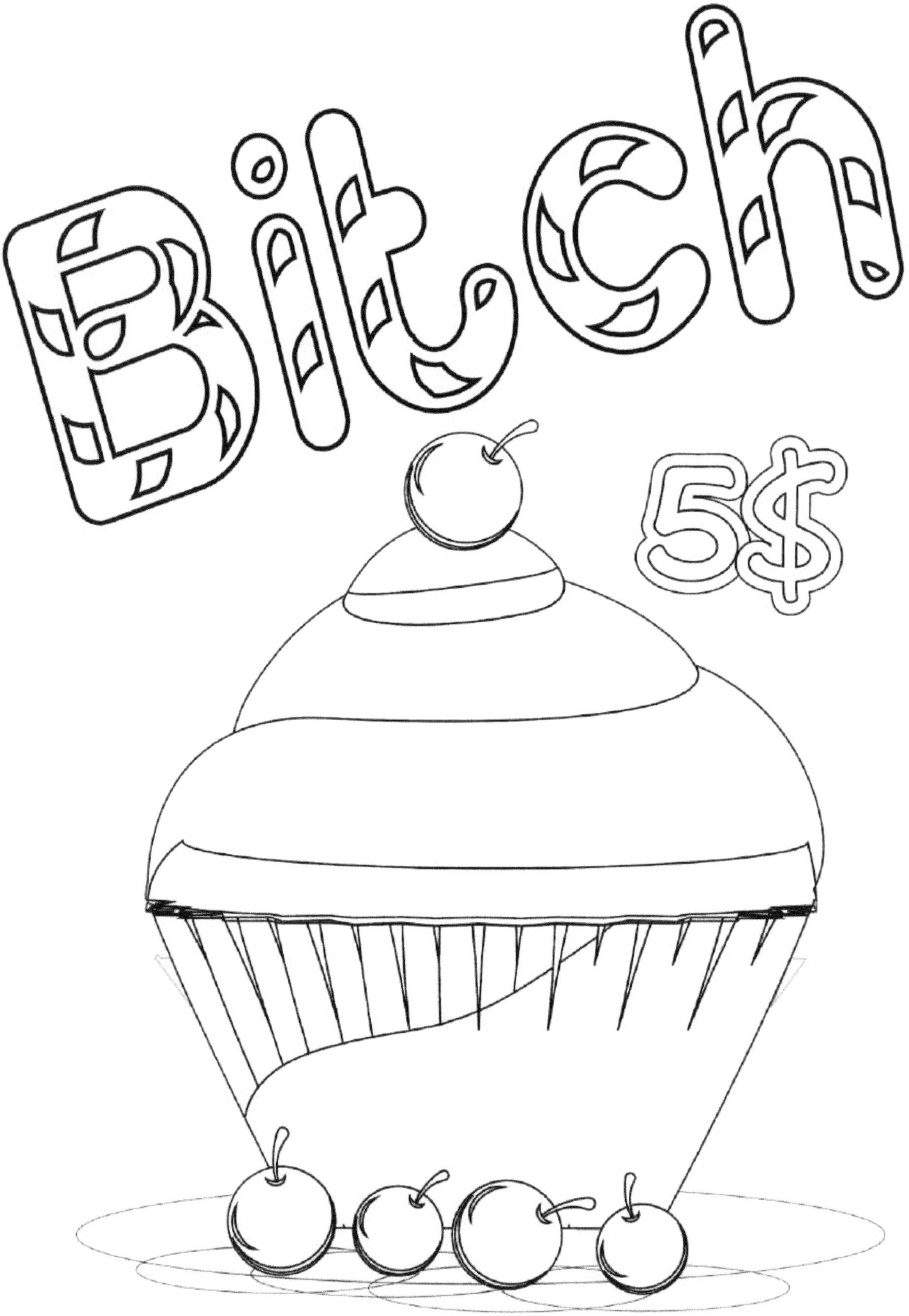
Bitch
5$

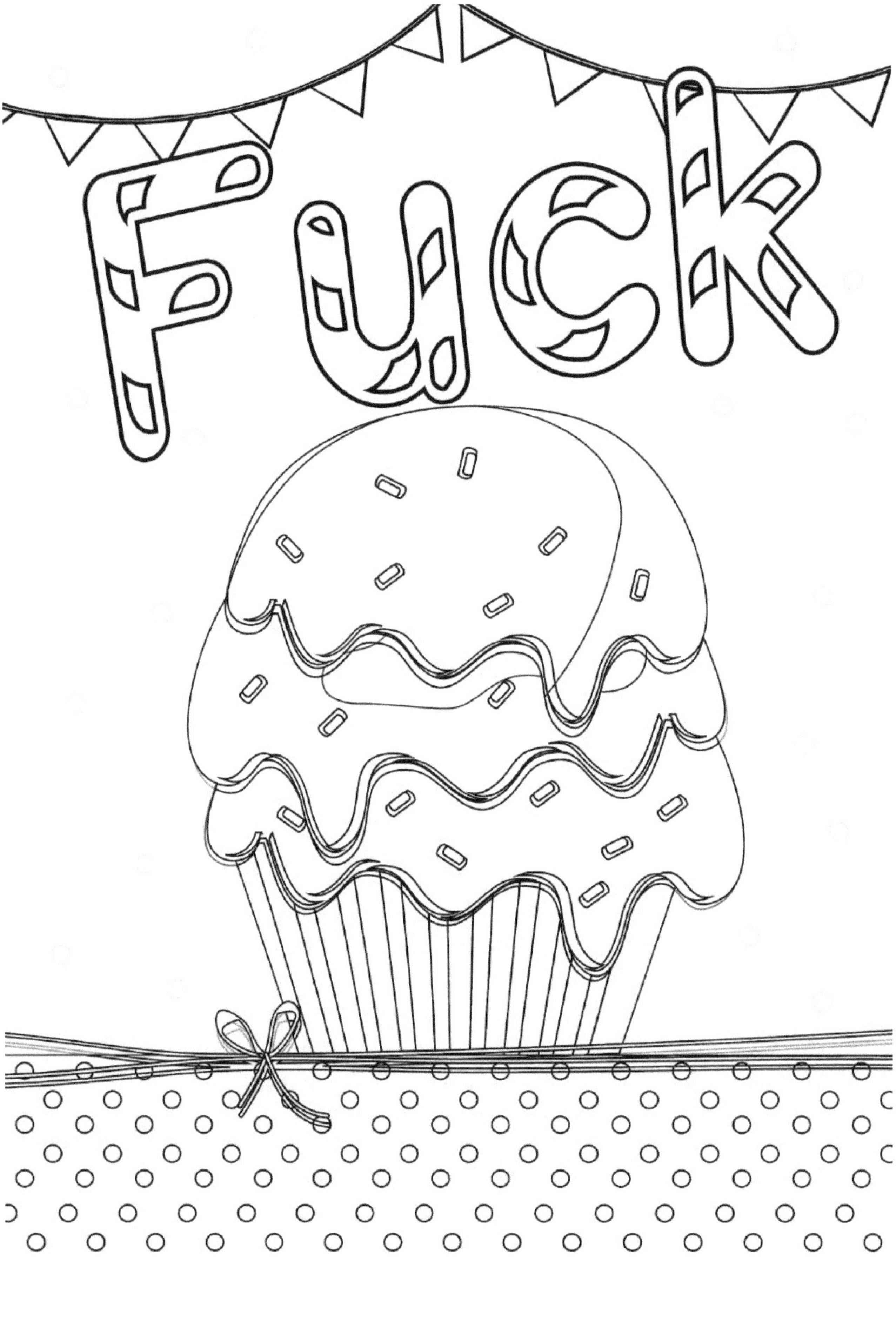
Fuck

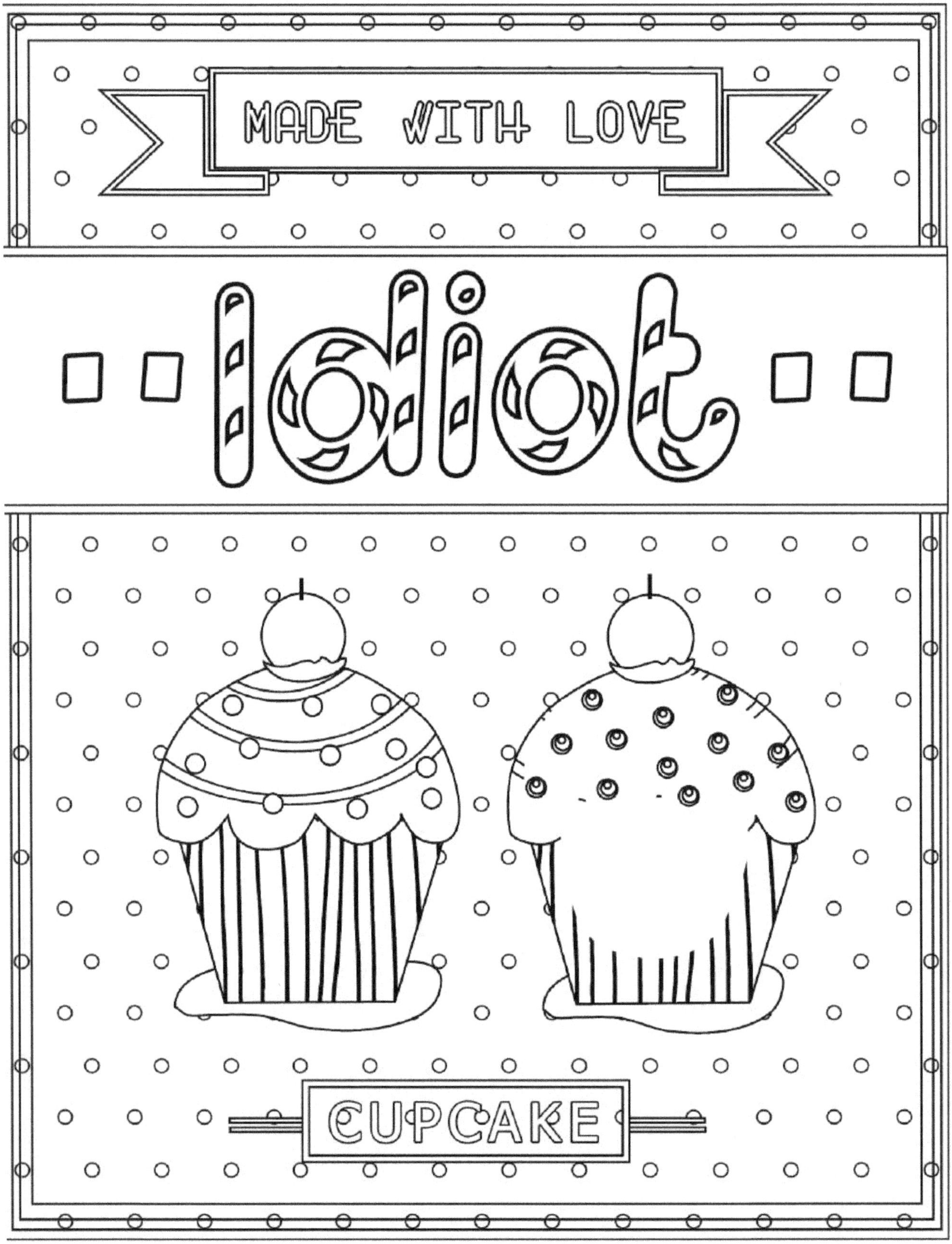
MADE WITH LOVE
idiot
CUPCAKE

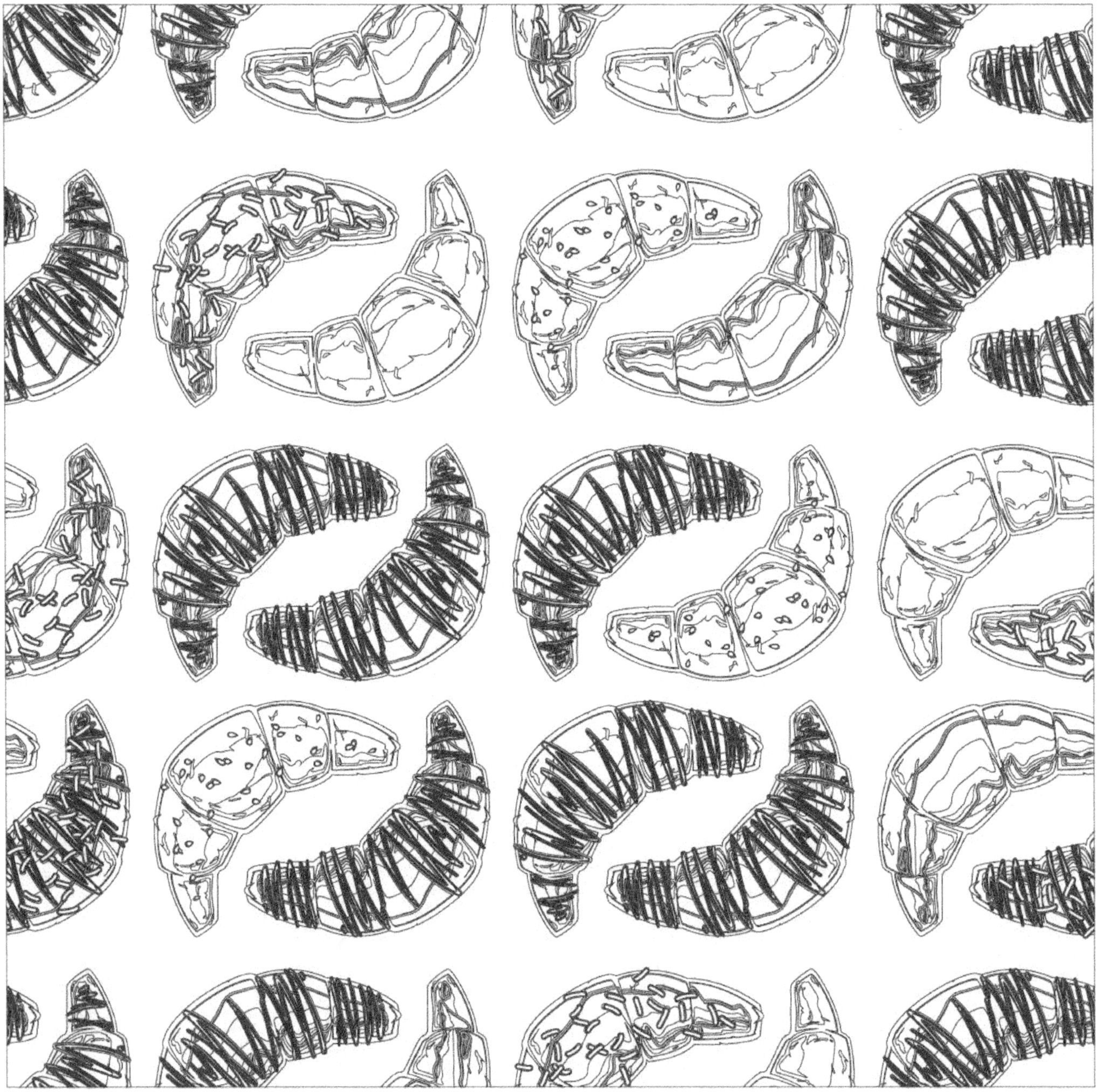

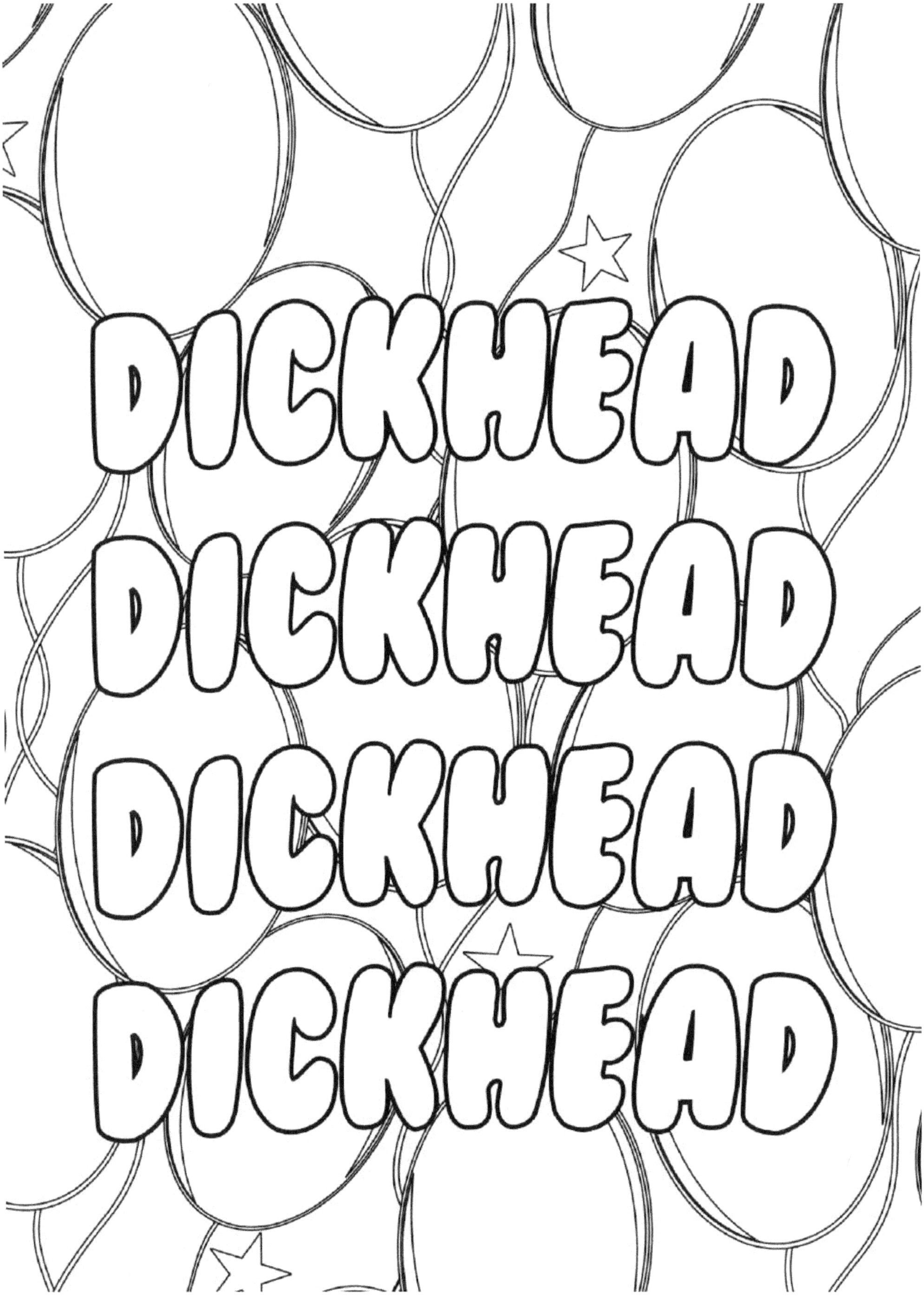
DICKHEAD
DICKHEAD
DICKHEAD
DICKHEAD

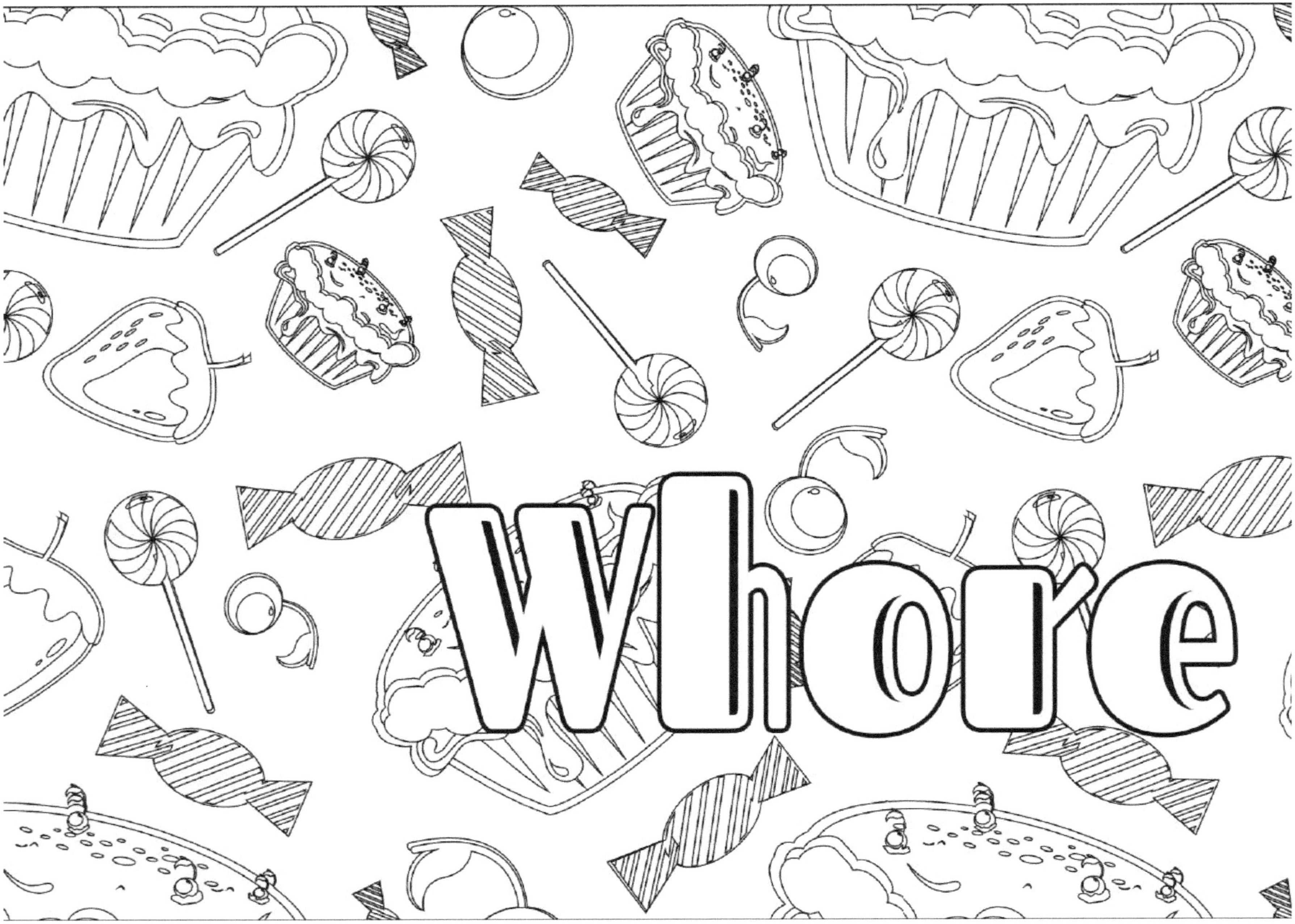
Whore

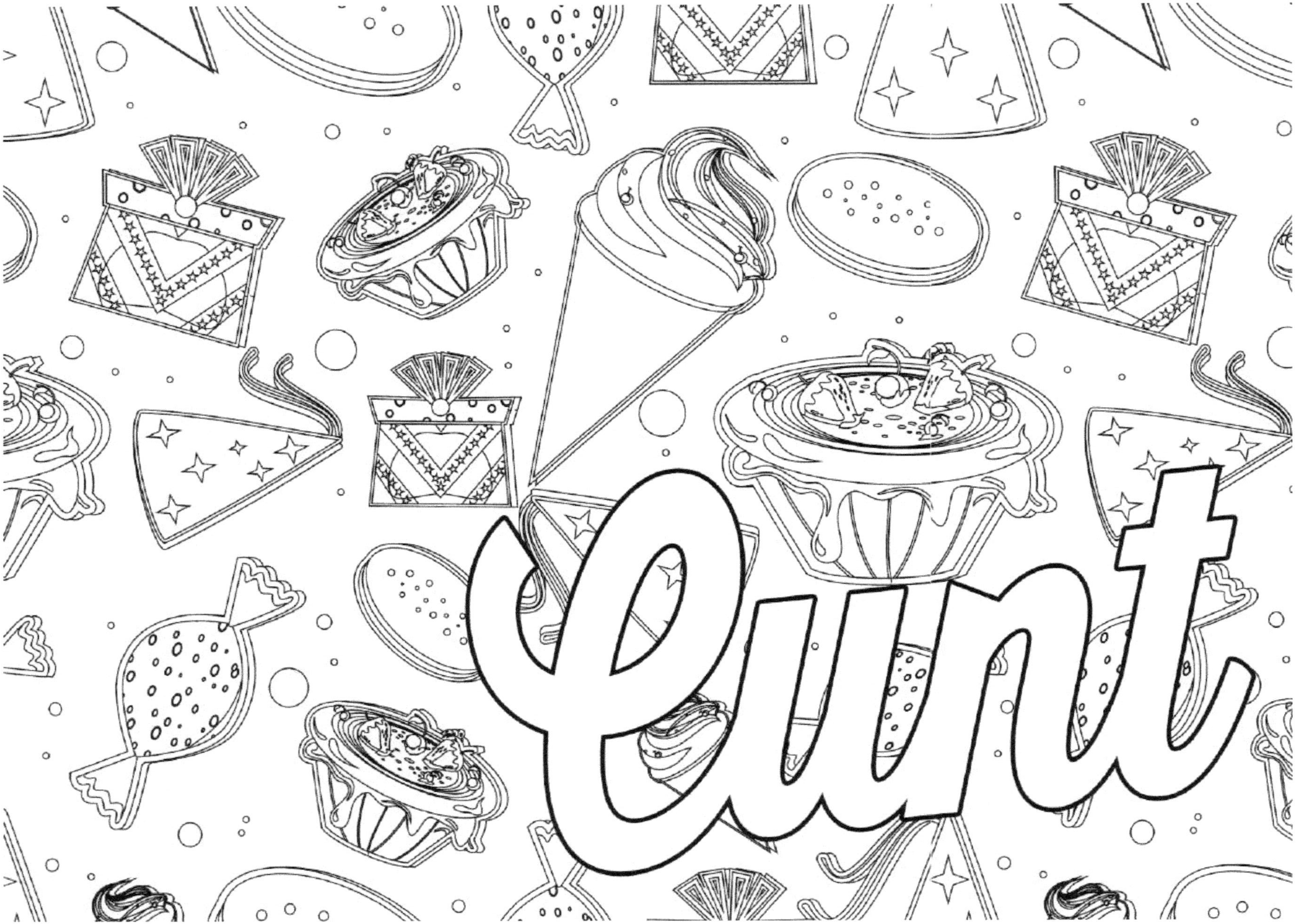
Cunt

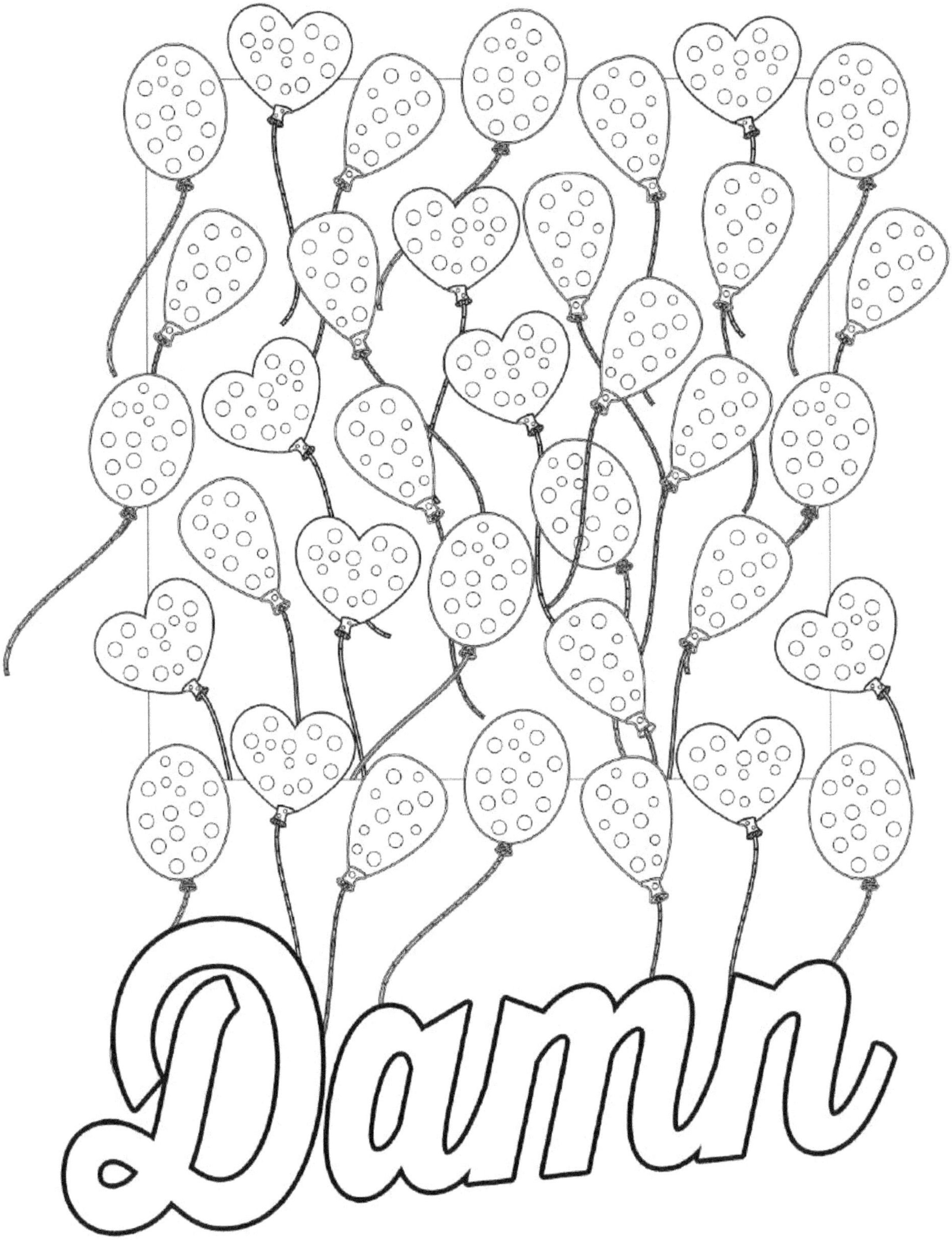
Damn

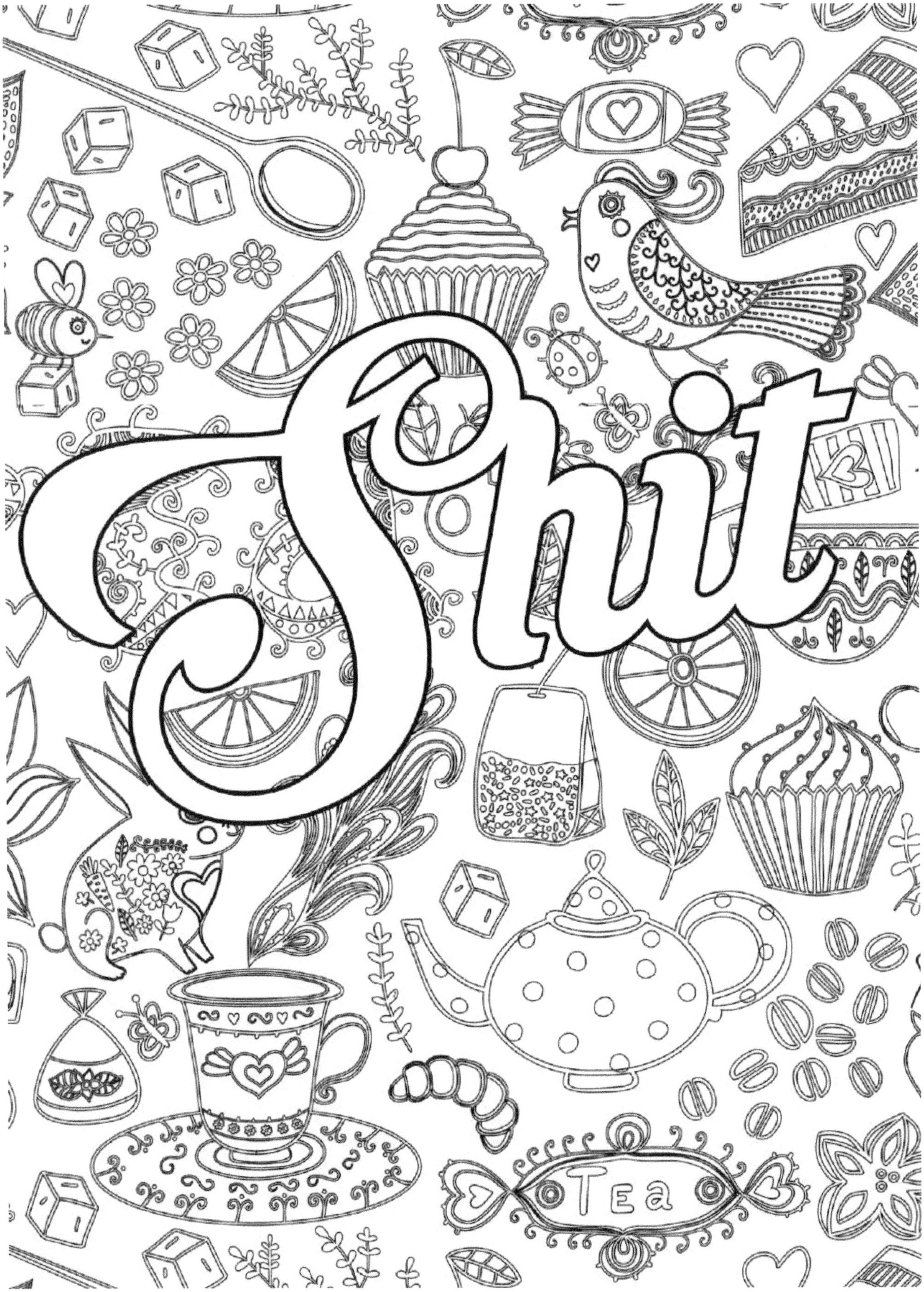
Shit
Tea

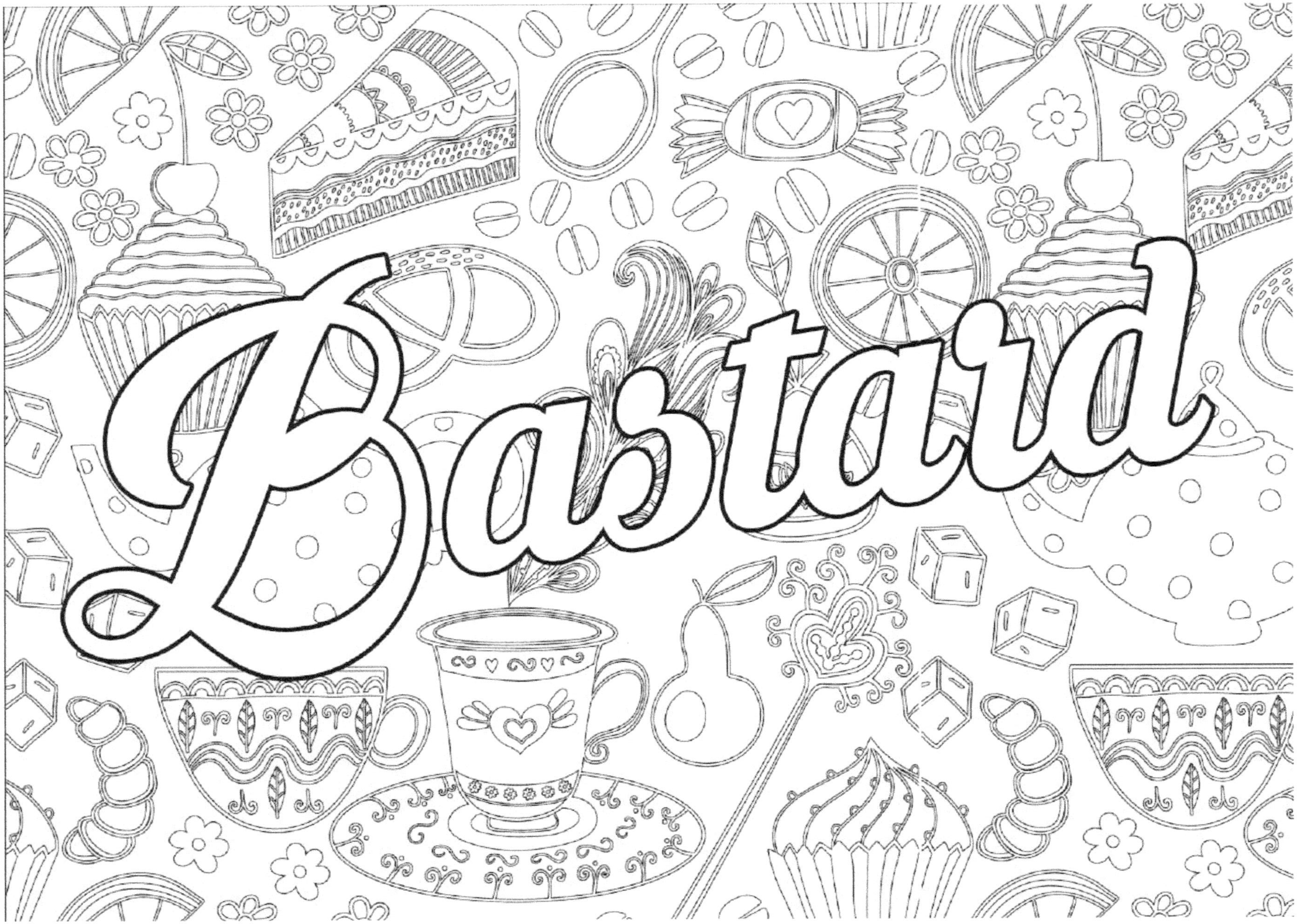
Bastard

DICKHEAD

Tea

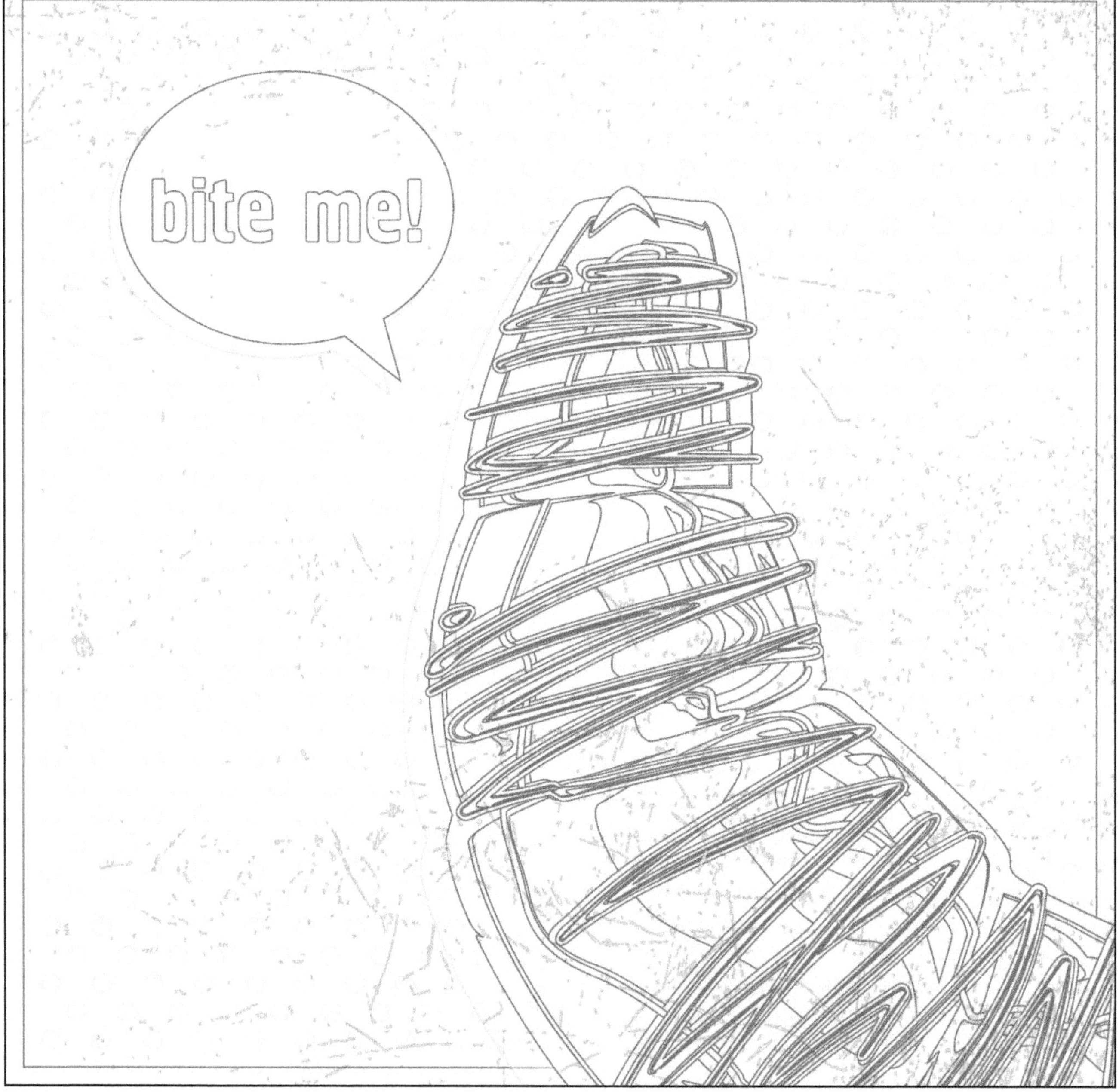
bite me!

www.ingramcontent.com/pod-product-compliance
Lightning Source LLC
Chambersburg PA
CBHW080601190526
45169CB00007B/2845
9781535179393